Let It Flow!

Writing for Wellness

JoAnn Streeter Shade

Let It Flow!

Writing for Wellness

JoAnn Streeter Shade

Gracednotes Ministries

Gracednotes Ministries

425 East Walnut Street

Ashland, Ohio 44805

gracednotesministries@gmail.com

Let It Flow! Writing for Wellness

ISBN-13: 978-1523379903

ISBN-10: 1523379901

Printed in the United States

With thanks to the Mental Health and Recovery Board of Ashland County

and the Margaret Clark Morgan Foundation

Welcome

One writes to make a home for oneself, on paper, in time, in others' minds.
Alfred Kazin

Welcome. These pages are designed to explore the world of words, of writing. They provide an overview of journaling, list-making, non-fiction development, story-telling, and poetry creation, set in the context of hope and healing for those who struggle with life issues, mental health concerns, and addictions. Scattered throughout these pages are nuggets of wisdom from veteran writers who offer advice, rules, tips, and other encouraging thoughts for the budding writer.

There are also a variety of writing exercises that provide prompts to get you started. You may want to write directly on these pages, or use the computer or a notebook. See what works for you. Perhaps you'll do some brainstorming on these pages, and then complete your poem or essay on the computer.

While this tool was initially created to be used in a writing workshop, it can be used individually, in a writers' group, with a writing coach, or in a therapeutic setting.

My hope is that as your words begin to flow, you will discover increased understanding, encouragement, and restoration.

Resistance knows that the longer we noodle around "getting ready," the more time and opportunity we'll have to sabotage ourselves. Resistance loves it when we hesitate, when we over-prepare. The answer: plunge in.
Steven Pressfield

Helpful Hints

No one is asking, let alone demanding, that you write.
The world is not waiting with bated breath for your article or book.
Whether or not you get a single word on paper, the sun will rise,
the earth will spin, the universe will expand.
Writing is forever and always a choice – your choice.
Beth Mende Conny

- You don't have to do any of the assignments on these pages. Not a one. What you have to do – if you want to write, to be a writer – is to write. So if you're writing nearly every day, even if it's greeting card verse or blog posts, you're just fine. If you're not – do the assignments.

- Take your time – this is not a test or a race. This is for you. Work at your own pace.

- Do what fits for you. Write, draw, or even find pictures from a magazine.

- Don't worry about spelling.

- Keep your words safe. Let others know these pages are private unless you choose to share them. Ask others to respect your privacy.

- If a particular writing assignment is hard for you or stirs up feelings that make you uncomfortable, feel free to move to another option. Skip it and come back to it later, or just let it go. Stop if you have to.

- Don't be afraid of the words.

- Talk with someone about what you're feeling – mad, sad, glad or scared. Share your concerns with your writing coach, a friend, or your therapist.

To create one's world in any of the arts takes courage.
Georgia O'Keeffe

Words to the Wise Would-Be Writer from Thrity Umrigar

1. Ask yourself why you want to write.

2. Ask yourself what you want to write.

3. Write in the shower.

4. Live a large and active life.

5. Be gentle with yourself. Great writing is always compassionate.

6. Read everything.

7. Write the story that haunts you.

8. Write for the right reasons. Write what's in your heart.

Find a subject you care about and which you in your heart feel others should care about.
It is this genuine caring, and not your games with language,
which will be the most compelling and seductive element in your style.
I am not urging you to write a novel, by the way – although I would not be sorry if you wrote one,
provided you genuinely cared about something.
A petition to the mayor about a pothole in front of your house or a love letter to the girl next door will do.
Kurt Vonnegut

Let It Rip

Journals

Life has a way of slipping away while we're not looking.
And many of us are so numbed by mundane routine that we hardly miss its passing.
Keeping a journal can bring back memories of those . . . timeless moments when the mists part.
Rare insights where you suddenly see your life from a new perspective.
Welcome moments when the pain subsides and the healing begins.
You'd think such moments would be unforgettable, but they are not. You will forget them.
They will quickly slip through your fingers if you don't tie them to your heart in a journal.
Luci Shaw

Getting Started

When I am invited to walk alongside people who are struggling with a variety of life issues, I often suggest the concept of keeping a journal. Some dive right in and benefit richly from the experience, but others look at me with the deer in the headlights glare, as though I'd suggested walking on hot coals as a therapeutic practice. No way are they going to write on a blank page.

The third response is the most common one. Yes, I'll try it, in fact I've always liked the idea of writing, but where do I start? What do I write?

In the counseling office, I began to provide prompts and other ideas to get people started. That process formed the basis for my first published book, *Heartwork of Hope: A Directed Journal*, providing guidance and direction for the person wanting to sort out issues such as how to determine their purpose in life, what integrity looked like for them, how relationships can be healed, and the role hope plays in the life of a person of faith.

As a disclaimer, this section does not constitute journal therapy, which is a model of counseling used by some therapists. Instead, it offers some helps for journal usage that can be therapeutic when used in conjunction with on-going therapy, group discussion, and/or self-reflection.

I write because I don't know what I think until I read what I say.
Flannery O'Connor

To Keep In Mind

Unlike poetry written in iambic pentameter (like sonnets), there are no rules in journal-writing. However, there are a few tips to guide the way:

There are no rules

It is a comforting reality that there is not a right way or wrong way to keep a journal.
Elizabeth O'Connor

Date each entry in your journal

Write whenever you like

Like the ground beneath your feet, your journal is always there to support your connection
to the world you live in.
Marlene A. Schiwy

Banish your internal editor

Write freely

Write fast, write everything, include everything, write from your feelings, write from your body,
accept whatever comes.
Tristine Ranier

Keep writing

Don't erase or cross-out any words.
Erasing just takes more time that you could be using to focus on you.

Write honestly

The keeping of a pilgrim journal requires a conscious, unswerving commitment to honesty with one's self.
Elizabeth O'Connor

Use color
Choose different colored pens or fonts to match your mood

Prompts

We'll start with prompts, sentence stems that may open the door to memories, hopes, and dreams. Here are a few of my favorite:

The season of the year that best describes me today is

A place where I find warmth is

In the last month, I have felt the most alive when

The time monster that is the hungriest in my day is

My body needs

One thing I could do in the days ahead to become the person I want to be is

It seems like my time is being eaten up by

In the silence, I am afraid

Nobody knows that I

Many questions are stirring in me just now

Mornings are

I am undecided about

The song that is stuck in my head

Write out three prompts of your own:

1.

2.

3.

Journal Entry #1

The season of the year that best describes me today is

Journal Entry #2

A place where I find warmth is

Journal Entry #3

In the last month, I have felt the most alive when

Journal Entry #4

The time monster that is the hungriest in my day is

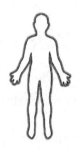

Journal Entry #5

My body needs

Journal Entry #6 (your choice)

Journal Entry #7 (your choice)

Therapeutic Journaling

The writers who get my personal award are the ones who show exceptional promise of looking at their lives in
this world as candidly and searchingly and feelingly as they know how and then of telling the rest of us what
they have found there most worth finding. We need the eyes of writers like that to see through.
We need the blood of writers like that in our vein.
Frederick Buechner

There are many ways that the use of a journal can aid mental health therapy. Entries can be made to document progress in therapy or to make note of what happened in a session. Writing can be assigned by the therapist to be completed in between sessions, and shared in therapy or kept private. Writing can also be used to reflect on aspects of mental health treatment and its aftermath. If you are in a continuing relationship with a mental health professional, you can use your journal entries as a springboard to the topics you bring to a session.

Henri Nouwen was a Catholic priest and educator who struggled with depression. His experience reminds us of the power of words when facing mental health struggles.

To my surprise, I never lost the ability to write.
In fact, writing became part of my struggle for survival.
It gave me the little distance from myself that I needed to keep from drowning in my despair.
Henri Nouwen

The following three journal entry options are specific to mental health diagnosis and its aftermath. Write about them if you so choose. Be sure to have a safety net in place, such as a caring friend, a peer counselor, your writing coach or group, a pastor or a mental health professional.

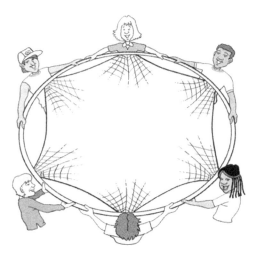

Therapeutic Journal Entry #1

When I think of my first psychiatric crisis and/or hospitalization, I remember

Therapeutic Journal Entry #2

Images of recovery take on many shapes and forms, such as a ten-lane interstate, a maze, a meandering path, a straight shot across the fairway, a quarter-mile track, a trail of crumbs through the woods, or a long and winding road (thank you, McCartney and Lennon). My recovery path

Therapeutic Journal Entry #3

When people learn that I have a mental health diagnosis,

As an Observer

Write about something that happened to you this week from the place of an observer. Instead of using "I," use "she" or "he." Describe the characters and the setting.

Write as an observer for five minutes.

An Unsent Letter

Write a letter you do not plan to send. Write to one of the following people:

Coach
High school teacher
Parent
Pastor
Therapist
Spouse or partner
Other person of significance

A Journal for Dreams

As early as the 10th century in Japan, "Pillow Books" were used to record daily lives and thoughts. One use of such books was to record dreams. What we know is that if a dream isn't spoken of, written of, or in some other way processed within ten minutes of waking, its message to us is often lost. For the next week, use a pillow book or scraps of paper to write down your dream(s) upon waking.

My Pillow Book of Dreams

Flow Writing

Start with a thought, feeling, idea or word. Write as long as you want, letting the words and ideas flow. Don't stop to correct or analyze anything. Try it out here, using one of the following words.

rope   peach   knee   cloud   rock

There are certain things which cannot be said, but they can be written.

Morning Pages

In *The Artist's Way*, Julia Cameron suggests that the bedrock tool of a creative recovery is a daily practice called Morning Pages. As described by Cameron,

Morning Pages are three pages of longhand, stream of consciousness writing, done first thing in the morning. There is no wrong way to do Morning Pages – they are not high art. They are not even "writing." They are about anything and everything that crosses your mind – and they are for your eyes only. Morning Pages provoke, clarify, comfort, cajole, prioritize and synchronize the day at hand. Do not over-think Morning Pages: just put three pages of anything on the page . . . and then do three more pages tomorrow.

Morning Pages can help to slice through brain loops, those thoughts that keep rewinding in your mind. They can aid in identifying what's important each day, and enable you to gain perspective over what happens to you. The discipline of Morning Pages can also help to establish new habits, and over time, they become the writer's preliminary stretches, similar to the warmups that athletes and dancers routinely do.

While writing every day sounds rather daunting, and does seem to break the rule of "no rules," it is a good way to get in the habit of writing on a regular basis, to get the words flowing and moving out of your head, onto the paper or computer screen. So give it a try for a couple of weeks and see how it works out for you.

Reading Your Journal

All this inner turmoil was, of course, hidden.
Between my face to the world and the inner pits of despair, there was no bridge of expression.
The habit of writing almost daily in my diary . . . probably saved my sanity.
If I could write out moods which could be admitted to no one, they became more manageable.
Anne Morrow Lindbergh

After you have finished a journal entry, take a walk or get up for a glass of water before you reread your entry, and remember to read your words with compassion. Try writing an Insight Line – one or two sentences about what your words are trying to tell you.

Insight line:

Insight line:

We shall not cease from exploration
And the end of all our exploring
Will be to arrive where we started
And know the place for the first time.
T.S. Elliot, The Four Quartets

Sort It Out

Lists

The list is the origin of culture. It's part of the history of art and literature. What does culture want? To make infinity comprehensible. It also wants to create order – not always, but often. And how, as a human being, does one face infinity? How does one attempt to grasp the incomprehensible? Through lists, through catalogs, through collections in museums and through encyclopedias and dictionaries.
Umberto Eco

Making Lists

I am a list-maker for two main reasons. The first is that it helps me to be organized, as I've been known to have a dozen projects going at one time. The second is that I feel really good when I cross something off my to-do list, so much so that I've been known to add something to my list that I've already accomplished, simply so I can have the pleasure of crossing it off.

Dr. Carrie Barron lists six reasons why lists are good for us.

1. Lists provide a positive psychological process whereby questions and confusions can be worked through. True purposes surface.

2. Lists foster a capacity to select and prioritize. This is useful for an information–overload situation.

3. Lists separate minutia from what matters, which is good for identity as well as achievement.

4. Lists help determine the steps needed. That which resonates informs direction and plan.

5. Lists combat avoidance. Taking abstract to concrete sets the stage for commitment and action, especially if you add self-imposed deadlines.

6. Lists organize and contain a sense of inner chaos which can make your load feel more manageable.

My Gratitude List

I am grateful for

1.

2.

3.

4.

5.

6.

7.

8.

9.

10.

11.

12.

13.

14.

15.

What does your gratitude list tell you about your life priorities? Do you need to thank anyone today who is on your gratitude list?

My Christmas Card List

I would like to send the following people a Christmas card this year.

1.

2.

3.

4.

5.

6.

7.

8.

9.

10.

11.

12.

13.

14.

15.

Is there a way you could be in touch with the people on your list throughout the year? What connection could you make this week?

My Reward List

When I accomplish something significant in my life, I would like to reward myself by

1.

2.

3.

4.

5.

6.

7.

8.

9.

10.

11.

12.

13.

14.

15.

How often do you reward yourself for an accomplishment? What could you do to pamper yourself today?

My Project List

I would like to complete the following projects this month

1.

2.

3.

4.

5.

6.

7.

8.

9.

10.

11.

12.

13.

14.

15.

What is the most doable project on your list? What is the most significant project on your list for your mental health?

Procrastinator's List

Here's a list that is similar to the "My Projects List." Julia Cameron suggests that most of us procrastinate when it comes to time. "We tell ourselves we don't have enough time to do X, an activity or undertaking that frightens us. The truth is that it is not our lack of time that is the issue, it is our lack of courage."

So for the Procrastinator's List, write down five tasks you've been procrastinating about, telling yourself you had "no time."

1.

2.

3.

4.

5.

Now take time in your own hands, and choose one task to cross off your list. One at a time, work through your whole list, proving to yourself that you *do* have time.

This week, I accomplished

My Bucket List

These are the things I want to do/accomplish before I'm 50, 60, 70, or before I kick the bucket

1.

2.

3.

4.

5.

6.

7.

8.

9.

10.

11.

12.

13.

14.

15.

Just for fun, rent The Bucket List with Jack Nicholson and Morgan Freeman. What's your favorite scene from the movie?

My Favorite Word List

Make a list of your favorite words, nouns, verbs, etc.

1.

2.

3.

4.

5.

6.

7.

8.

9.

10.

11.

12.

13.

14.

15.

16.

17.

18.

19.

20.

Check back to this list when you're working on the poetry section.

My List of 100

Use one of the following to complete a list of 100 – repeats are fine. Make sure to do it all at one time. No answer is a bad answer.

100 things I like/value about myself
100 things I like
100 things I don't like
100 things I want to change
100 things I want to do
100 fears I have
100 things I miss

1.

2.

3.

4.

5.

6.

7.

8.

9.

10.

11.

12.

13.

14.

15.

16.

17.

18.

19.

20.

21.

22.

23.

24.

25.

26.

27.

28.

29.

30.

31.

32.

33.

33.

34.   58.

35.   59.

36.   60.

37.   61.

38.   62.

39.   63.

40.   64.

41.   65.

42.   66.

43.   67.

44.   68.

45.   69.

46.   70.

47.   71.

48.   72.

49.   73.

50.   74.

51.   75.

52.   76.

53.   77.

54.   78.

55.   79.

56.   80.

57.   81.

82.

83.

84.

85.

86.

87.

88.

89.

90.

91.

92.

93.

94.

95.

96.

97.

98.

99.

100

.

What's repeated a number of times on your list?

What do the patterns tell you?

What has this list shown you about yourself?

A "Just For Fun" List

Keri Smith compiled a list of 100 ideas to use with a journal. Here are just a few.

1. Go for a walk. Draw or list things you find on the sidewalk.

2. Take fifteen minutes to eat an orange.

3. Trace your footsteps with chalk.

4. Hang upside down for five minutes.

5. Study the face of someone you do not like.

6. List ten of your habits.

7. Give away something you love.

8. Make a useful item using only paper and tape.

9. Find a photo. Alter it by drawing over it.

10. Record all the sounds you hear in the course of an hour.

11. Create an image using dots.

12. Write a list of all the things you do to escape.

13. Write about or draw some of the doors in your life.

14. Illustrate the concept of simplicity.

15. Recall a favorite childhood game.

A List of Tips for Getting Organized to Write

1. Work with yourself, not against yourself.
2. Understand your strengths.
3. Focus and pay attention.
4. Invest your time.
5. Create habits.
6. Use the right tools.
7. Work forward.

Convince Me

Non-Fiction

To be persuasive we must be believable;
to be believable we must be credible;
to be credible we must be truthful.
Edward R. Murrow

Non-Fiction

Non-fiction can take a variety of forms, including copying a traditional recipe, composing an effective letter-to-the-editor, writing a persuasive column or blog post, completing a term paper or dissertation, or developing a lengthy book on a particular subject. Autobiographies and memoirs are also non-fiction. This section will focus on writing non-fiction that expresses an opinion of some kind.

What do we write about? In her book, *Writing to Change the World*, Mary Pipher gives us some suggestions:

- What makes you laugh, cry, and open your heart?

- What points do you repeatedly make to those you love?

- What topics keep you up at night, or help you fall asleep?

- What do you know to be true?

- What do you consider to be evil?

- What is beautiful to you?

- What do you most respect in others?

- What excites your curiosity?

- What do you want to accomplish before you die?

Words are sacred.
They deserve respect.
If you get the rights ones, in the right order, you can nudge the world a little.
Tom Stoppard

Autobiography in Six Words.

Here's a fun yet challenging writing exercise to start this section. A number of years ago, *Smith Magazine* introduced the memoir or autobiography in six words. Available on the magazine's website, these have been published in book form, *Not Quite What I Was Planning*, edited by Rachel Fershleiser and Larry Smith. Here are some examples, with authors noted when known:

Seventy years, few tears, hairy ears. (Bill Querengesser)

Catholic school backfired. Sin is in!   (Nikki Beland)

Born in the desert, still thirst. (Georgene Nunn)

Please do not sit on me.

I still make coffee for two. (Zak Nelson)

Sounded much better in my head.

Moved every year then came home. (Allison Harris)

No future, no past. Not lost. (Matt Brensilver)

Almost a victim of my family. (Chuck Sangster)

Extremely responsible, secretly longed for spontaneity. (Sabra Jennings)

It's simpler than they tell you. (Josh Kruger)

That evening the sun didn't set. (Zoe Stoller)

Tips from Beth Carter for the Six Word Autobiography

1.   Choose six compelling word. Be selective.

2.   Use punctuation to your advantage.

3.   Eliminate needless words.

4.   Choose a theme.

5.   Write a good story.

My Autobiography in Six Words

Give it a try.

1.

2.

3.

Write even when the world is chaotic.
You don't need a cigarette, silence, music, a comfortable chair, or inner peace to write.
You just need ten minutes and a writing implement.
Cory Doctorow

This I Believe

I have forced myself to begin writing when I've been utterly exhausted,
when I've felt my soul as thin as a playing card,
when nothing has seemed worth enduring for another five minutes . . .
and somehow the activity of writing changes everything.
Or appears to do so.
Joyce Carol Oates

This I Believe is an international organization engaging people in writing and sharing essays describing the core values that guide their daily lives. Further information is found at the thisibelieve.org website.

Here are the guidelines their website provides as guidance to writing a statement of personal belief:

Tell a story about you. Be specific. Take your belief out of the ether and ground it in the events that have shaped your core values. Make sure your story ties to the essence of your daily life philosophy and the shaping of your beliefs.

Be brief. A statement should be 500-600 words, about three minutes when read aloud.

Name your belief. If you can't name it in a sentence or two, the essay may not be about belief.

Be positive. Write about what you do believe. Avoid statements of religious dogma, preaching, or editorializing.

Be personal. Make your essay about you; speak in the first person.

Possible themes are family, marriage, truth, gratitude, responsibility, integrity, legacy, humility, pleasure, purpose, creativity, and courage.

Here are a few titles of the more popular essays:
The choice to be stronger
The best kind of grief is gratitude
The power to connect
I shall overcome my fears
I believe in laughter
The perfume of love

This I Believe

Theme:

Premise in one sentence:

Story or image:

My essay:

In My Opinion

In fiction, when you paint yourself into a corner, you can write a pair of suction cups onto the bottoms of your shoes and walk up the wall and out the skylight and see the sun breaking through the clouds.
In nonfiction, you don't have that luxury.
Tom Robbins

Traditionally, newspaper columns have been ways in which a writer could express his or her opinion on a variety of subjects. While these opportunities still exist, social media, blogs, and website articles now provide other options for the budding writer. Here are some tips on writing an effective and persuasive opinion piece.

1. Consider the audience, purpose, content and structure before writing.
2. Write about people. Tell the story through experiences of local people.
3. Begin with an opening "lead" to catch the interest of the reader.
4. Be timely.
5. Vary the material instead of writing on one subject.
6. Avoid difficult or technical words, long sentences and long paragraphs.
7. Stimulate curiosity in your subject.

Here's a sample newspaper column that begins with the idea of writing a newspaper column:

I'm sometimes asked how I go about writing a newspaper column. In the "where do you get your ideas" category, I don't have the little boy handing up ideas from the cellar like Anne Lamott describes. I simply listen and watch and observe, and lo and behold, there's an idea for a column. So far I haven't run out, but you may have noticed that I am writing about writing a column.

A second question is about process. When you sit down to write a column, do you have it all planned out (like a doctoral dissertation where you know before you start that chapter 4 will be a statistical analysis of your findings)? Well, no – I never quite know where I'll end up when I start, and sometimes am pleasantly surprised to see that I've actually strung together 700 words that somehow fit.

Yet today, I managed to plot out the whole column in my head as I observed the Sabbath (at least the two hours after the roast chicken dinner) on the couch of our living room/office. Now if I can only remember it . . .

The prompt came over the course of this past weekend. I spent it in three separate settings with three incredible women – a New Testament scholar, a marriage and family therapist/seminary professor, and an ethicist. These women are definitely specialists – they have a unique niche in the academic world and are exceptionally skilled in that niche.

As often happens when I am in connection with women like that, I began that internal whine that weaves notes of envy and "what if" through the muzak echoing in my head. My chosen profession (or the calling that chose me, to be more exact), is that of a generalist. As a Salvation Army officer, I function in a variety of 'jack-of-all-trades' roles. I suppose that the official ones would be pastor and administrator, but this past week I've done two stints as receptionist, worked in the concession stand at the Kroc Center, vacuumed the carpets and tweaked the budget. And that's just my day (and sometimes night) job.

But I am also a writer. I used to say, I'm a Salvation Army officer who writes, but I've finally grown into this writer garment enough to claim this additional identity. Yes, I am a Writer. I've had two books published, a third is in the pipeline, and I'm also a regular columnist for the Ashland Times-Gazette. There, I said it out loud. Just the fact that I write something nearly every day should in itself qualify me as a writer, but I guess that in my mind, the fact that people actually read what I write allows me to move to the capital "W."

So here's my dilemma. I am firmly entrenched in midlife, even beginning to push the upper limits of that category, and retirement from my vocation is not too many years away. It's not too early to dream of what I'll be when I grow up, and wonder, could I be a Writer in my retirement years? If so, the experts tell me, I'd better get ready now. I need to define my core message, establish a brand, blog regularly, network, twitter, and find my unique voice.

But wait a minute. I'm not sure about this core message and branding stuff. I like writing about grief and mother-of-the-groom dresses, Ashland high school football and the devastation in Haiti. And I like writing because I want to, not because I have to. I want to hold onto Brenda Ueland's image of writing, "a child stringing beads in kindergarten – happy, absorbed and quietly pulling one bead on after another."

So maybe I don't want to be a specialist after all. While the juggling can get a bit intense, I like a life with many facets. Like the women of the Harlem Renaissance, I can try my hand at many things – and dream in color at the same time. I like beads that are multi-hued, round, square and even misshapen, and was glad to string one more jewel on my necklace this afternoon. Thanks for asking – and for reading.

Choose one of the following topics (or one of your own) and write 500-700 words about it.
Presidential debates
Community-based mental health services are
Product names: dirty chips, honest tea

My Opinion

The Personal Essay and Memoir

The nonfiction story, after all, isn't really about dying mom. It's about the writer and how she did or did not deal with dying mom . . . Dying mom is a Big Deal, but without plunging the depth, without any kind of evidence of movement in the narrator (writer, person, life of writer), there is nothing for the reader here, except maybe pity. The Big Question for all essayists and memoirists is a pursuit to know thyself (as Steven Harvey and Greek philosophers say), not record for friends and family an extended account of mom dying, however unique or unusual that death is. The fact is, everyone dies, and it doesn't matter what happened... it only matters what large sense the writer makes of what happened (as Vivian Gornick says). There has to be progression from "This happened, and I hated it," to "and here's what I made of it."

Sarah Wells

Choose one of the following memoir prompts and write for five minutes:

What clique did you belong to in school?

What is your happiest childhood memory?

What is your first memory of trauma?

What was the first moment you felt grown-up or independent?

When did you first feel powerless?

What regrets do you have?

Rules for Writing by Natalie Goldberg

1. Keep your hand moving.

2. Lose control.

3. Be specific.

4. Don't think.

5. Don't worry about punctuation, spelling, or grammar.

6. You are free to write the worst junk in America.

7. Go for the jugular.

The secret to finishing a manuscript: Bum Glue.

Making It Up

Story-Telling
(aka Fiction)

I find interesting characters or lessons that resonate with people and sometimes I write about them on the sports pages, sometimes I write them in a column, sometimes in a novel, sometimes a play or sometimes in nonfiction. But at the core I always say to myself, 'Is there a story here? Is this something people want to read?'
Mitch Albom

Components of Fiction

Novel writing goes, at its best, beyond cleverness to that point where one's whole mind and experience and vision are the novel and the effort to translate this wholeness into prose is the life: a circle of creation.
Gore Vidal

While there are various ways to organize the parts of story-telling, there are generally six main components to the art of fiction:

- Setting

- Characters

- Plot

- Point of View

- Theme

- Style

On the following pages, you will find descriptions, guiding questions, and exercises to explore how to develop the various parts of story-telling, whether it be in the form of short stories or a novel.

Writing Instructions from Anne Lamott

1. Write regularly.
2. Give yourself short assignments.
3. Write sh**ty first drafts.
4. Let the Polaroid develop.
5. Know your characters.
6. Let the plot grow out of the characters.
7. Have pen and paper ready at all times.
8. Call around. Ask for help.
9. Write in your own voice.
10. Devotion and commitment will be their own reward.

Setting

The great writers keep writing about the cold dark place within, the water under a frozen lake or the secluded, camouflage hole. The light they shine on this hole, this pit, helps us cut away or step around the brush and brambles, then we can dance around the rim of the abyss, holler into it, measure it, throw rocks in it, and still not fall in. It can no longer swallow us up. And we can get on with things.
Toni Morrison.

Description: The setting of a story or novel describes where and when the action takes place. The setting can be large (New York City) or small (a hospital ward, a booth at a favorite restaurant). Setting also includes the year and the season.

Guiding Questions: Where, when, and (under) what circumstances? What cultural content (if any)?

Exercise: Write a description of your bedroom.

Exercise: Choose a setting and write a character sketch for it. What is its personality, style, attitude, class and philosophy? Is it dark or light, relaxed or stressed? Does it swallow people up or embrace them?

Characters

If your deepest beliefs drive your writing, they will not only keep your work from being contrived but will help you discover what drives your characters.
Anne Lamott

Description: Characters are the people, animals, and other beings that are present in the story. They may be flat, one-dimensional characters, or round, complex, and fully developed. Some characters are static, staying the same from beginning to end, while others are dynamic, changing over the course of the story. You may choose stock characters, such as the archetypal western hero or witch, or a stereotype, such as a dumb blonde or a silly teenager. A universal character is one who has the problems and traits that are common to all, while an individual would be more eccentric or have an unusual combination of characteristics (such as in science fiction).

Guiding Questions: Who is the main character in the story? If a character was missing, would the story lose its power? Will the reader be glad to see your characters go at the end of the story, or disappointed they won't meet again?

Exercise: Use this opening line. "I was born on February 29th . . .

Exercise: Write a speech in which your character describes his/her experience of discovering a dead body.

Exercise: Your character has a deep, dark secret. Today is the day to reveal that secret. What is it? Who does he or she reveal it to? What is the reaction?

Plot

Writing, in itself, is like the sound of one hand clapping – incomplete, silent, and without impact.
Only when the writer as the one hand, and the reader as the other, confront each other, is there that clap,
that spark of communication which makes literature alive.
Minfong Ho

Description: The plot of the story is the action (or lack of action) that moves the reader from point A to point B. It can be outlined as the sequence of major events.

Guiding Questions: What happens in the story? What is the design (structure) – time line – of the narrative?

Exercise: Develop the story you plan to write in one sentence. State what the main character wants more than anything else in life. List three obstacles to keep his from reaching his goal. Make a timeline for the events of the novel. Make a map that shows where the action will take place.

One sentence:

Main character's desire:

Three obstacles:

Timeline or map:

Exercise: Your main character is Shelly. Her overall objective is to get married. Her scene objective is to get Kyle, whom she has just met in a coffee shop, to ask her for a date. Write the scene from Shelly's point of view.

Exercise: Zizi and Zulie are miniature dachshunds. One day they dig their way under the fence and escape into the next door neighbor's garden. The neighbor is an old woman. What happens next?

Point of View

Anything you do not give freely and abundantly becomes lost to you.
You open the door of your safe and you find ashes.
Annie Dillard

Description: Who is telling the story? Is it a sympathetic narrator, the main character, or someone on the margin of the action? Point of view can be first person (I) or third person (she, he, it). If third person, is the story seen through the eyes and understanding of one person, or does the reader get a glimpse of each character's view? Is your narrator reliable? Is the narrator objective or prejudiced? Some novels switch back and forth between the various voices of their characters.

Guiding Question: Who is telling the story?

Exercise: A teenage couple is sitting on a park bench, making up a love test for each other. What are the questions? Write about their conversation. Now, write the scene as if the couple has been married for twenty-five years.

Exercise: It's recognition night at the football game, where the high school seniors walk across the field with their parents and are honored for their participation. Write a paragraph about this from four points of view: the student, a parent, the football coach with cancer, and a father in the stands whose son died five years before from a football related injury.

Exercise: Write about a past family gathering or the most embarrassing thing that ever happened in your high school. Write in detail, explaining what you saw, what you did, and how you felt. Then rewrite the same story from the perspective of someone else.

Style

Long before I wrote stories, I listened for stories.
Eudora Welty

Description: Style is the fingerprint of the story, the novel. This doesn't necessarily get determined in the beginning; rather, it will emerge in the writing through the diction (choice of words), syntax (arrangement of words) and the voice used.

Guiding Questions: Does the finished work have a unique feel? How would you describe that?

Exercise: A woman is walking when she trips and almost falls. When she looks around, she sees that a man is smiling at her. Describe this situation in four different ways, using a change of tone, sentence structure, style, tension, voice, but maintain the same setting and characters. Possible tones are humorous, snarky, uppity, emotional, bitter, or bored.

#1

#2

#3

#4

Theme

You write to expose the unexposed.
If there is one door in the castle you have been told not to go through, you must.
Otherwise, you'll just be rearranging furniture in rooms you've already been in.
Most human beings are dedicated to keeping that one door shut. But the writer's job is to see what's behind it,
to see the bleak unspeakable stuff, and to turn the unspeakable into words —
not just into any words but if we can, into rhythm and blues.
Anne Lamott

Description: Each story, whether two pages or two hundred pages, needs to have a theme, a Big Idea. Some possibilities are betrayal, love, friendship, family, honor, justice, and grief. At its conclusion, it may be summarized by, "and the moral of the story is . . ."

Guiding Questions: Why did this writer bring these characters to this place at this time? What is the point? What do readers now know, [should] understand?

Exercise: Write about a time when you accomplished something you thought you couldn't do.

Exercise: Using revenge as a theme, write two paragraphs about a woman who lost her job because she was a whistleblower.

It's in the Details

Writing nonfiction is more like sculpture, a matter of shaping the research into the finished thing.
Novels are like paintings, specifically watercolors.
Every stroke you put down you have to go with.
Of course you can rewrite, but the original strokes are still there in the texture of the thing.
Joan Didion

Can the reader connect with the story? Often, that connection is made through the details, the descriptions that draw upon the five senses.

Exercise: On an airline flight, what are five things you might see?

Five things you might hear?

Five things you might smell?

Five things you might touch?

Five things you might taste?

Five emotions you might experience?

Story Ideas

Idea #1 Combine a stolen ring, a fear of spiders and a sinister stranger into the following short story idea. A babysitter is snooping around her employer's house and finds a disturbing photograph.

Idea #2 Combine an annoying boss, a bikini, and a fake illness into the following short story idea. Your character's boss invites her and her husband to dinner. Your character wants to make a good impression, but her husband has a tendency to drink too much and say exactly what's on his mind.

Idea #3 Make a list of five things you're afraid of happening to you. Then write a story in which one of them happens to your character.

Idea #4 What is one of your bad habits? Invent a character who has that bad habit, but a much worse case of it than you have. Write a story where this habit gets your character into trouble.

Idea #5 Grandpa should not be driving. But no one dares to hide the car keys. Write the scene . . .

Advice from *On Writing* by Stephen King

1. Stop watching television. Instead, read as much as possible.

2. Prepare for more failure and criticism than you think you can deal with.

3. Don't waste time trying to please people.

4. Write primarily for yourself.

5. Disconnect from the rest of the world while writing.

6. Don't be pretentious.

7. Avoid adverbs and long paragraphs.

8. Don't get overly caught up in grammar.

9. Master the art of description.

10. Don't give too much background information.

11. Tell stories about what people actually do.

12. Take risks; don't play it safe.

13. Take your writing seriously.

14. Write every day.

15. When you're finished writing, take a long step back.

16. Have the guts to cut.

Let It Rhyme
(or Not)

Poetry

Poetry is when an emotion has found its thought and the thought has found words.
Robert Frost

Poetry and Prose

What's the difference between poetry and prose? Merriam-Webster tells us that poetry is "writing that formulates a concentrated imaginative awareness of experience in language chosen and arranged to create a specific emotional response through meaning, sound and rhythm." Lots of words to describe a poem.

I prefer to use the images of the poets to help us understand what makes the poetic speak to us. Joseph Roux suggests that "Poetry is truth in its Sunday clothes," while Carl Sandburg describes poetry as "an echo, asking a shadow to dance." Often, poetry is said to take the ordinary and turn it on its head. Unlike the action of fiction or the persuasion of nonfiction, Maxine Kumin tells us that "Poetry makes nothing happen, it survives in the valley of its saying." Robert Frost described it, "Like a piece of ice on a hot stove, the poem must ride on its own melting," while Dennis Gabor understands that "Poetry is plucking at the heartstrings, and making music with them."

Poetry is what in a poem makes you laugh, cry, prickle, be silent, makes your toe nails twinkle, makes you want to do this or that or nothing, makes you know that you are alone in the unknown world, that your bliss and suffering is forever shared and forever all your own.
Dylan Thomas

Poetry isn't a profession, it's a way of life.
It's an empty basket: you put your life into it and make something out of that.
Mary Oliver

We're going to approach poetry writing in two ways. First, we'll do a couple of exercises to help our brains switch into poetic gear through the use of a poetry pentad and a childhood image exercise.

When we've completed those exercises, we'll try our hand at a few forms of poetry, including the acrostic, the limerick, the haiku, the cinquain, nonsense poems, and free verse.

A Poetry Pentad

John Timpane (*Poetry for Dummies*) suggests the following exercise to utilize the five major poetic principles — attentiveness, concentration (of language, insight, and emotion), originality, experimentation, and form.

Step #1: Write down a very mundane, straightforward prose statement about the outside world. You could write about a cut on your hand, a kiss, awkward silences, or a cash machine that won't give you any money. Write something as simple as, "Sure is a nice sunset."

Step #2: Pay closer attention to the thing you just wrote about. Write down what you notice. Brainstorm. List as many aspects as you can: "The color of the sunset is red in some places and a flat grayish-blue in others. The sky nearer to the sun is pretty, but farther away some of it is already dark and colorless."

Step #3: Concentrate on your subject and come up with a few new ways of presenting or describing the thing your original statement was about. Try using some metaphors, images, turns of phrase. Don't write down anything you've ever heard or read before. Reject anything that seems familiar or secondhand. Using the sunset as your subject, you could write, "The sunset is like a bruise; it's like spilled stew on a rug; it's a molten core with a hard outer crust."

Step #4: Write at least two passages of poetry on this subject, experimenting with different forms. Choose very different forms (say, two lines that rhyme with each other, or a passage of free verse, which doesn't have any rhyme). For example, two rhyming lines about the sunset

Blood-red, flat grey, the sunset colors fuse,
Spreading and growing dull green, like a bruise

Free verse:

The sunset spilled over the rug of the sky seeped into its fabric
A stain spread, a ravishing mess will leave a mark
No way I can cleanse it from my absorbent brain.
It's running down the corners, lava hardening, darkening, losing light. It's nighttime.

Step #5: Rewrite one of the passages in as few words as you can. Go for maximum meaning and emotion. For example:

Sunset spilled on the rug, stained the fabric, can't get it out of my brain. It's lava, hardening to darkness.

Pentad Attempt #1

Step #1: Write a prose statement

Step #2: Brainstorm images and ideas

Step #3: Determine a new expression

Step #4: Create two different poems

Step #5: Rewrite and refine

Pentad Attempt #2

Step #1: Write a prose statement

Step #2: Brainstorm images and ideas

Step #3: Determine a new expression

Step #4: Create two different poems

Step #5: Rewrite and refine

Pentad Attempt #3

Step #1: Write a prose statement

Step #2: Brainstorm images and ideas

Step #3: Determine a new expression

Step #4: Create two different poems

Step #5: Rewrite and refine

Childhood Images

Here's an idea from John Fox, writing in *Poetic Medicine: The Healing Art of Poem-Making*.

Start by making a list of images from your childhood. Pick the ones with a positive feeling for you. Treat them like snapshots you might look through after many years.

Recall the ways you felt in your body – what you saw, smelled, heard, felt and tasted. Absorb the image into your body – feel as if you are reliving the remembered image. If you're working with a partner, describe your experience briefly. If you're working alone, speak of your experience out loud.

Next, write down the emotions associated with these images, thinking of the broad categories of mad, sad, glad and scared.

Write a poem using the details you've collected. It can be rhymed, free verse, haiku, or even a limerick. Stay in touch with your senses as you focus on your image, as you listen for the voice of the image, and then as you express what you are feeling. Show the feelings in your poem instead of labeling it as happy or sad.

Image Exercise

Step #1: Make a list of childhood images

Step #2 Choose a positive image

Step #3 Remember what that felt like: sight, touch, taste, hearing, smell

Step #4 List emotions that arise from that image

Step #5 Write a few lines of poetry to connect the image, the body memories, and the emotions

Poetry Tools

Line Breaks: writing in shorter lines to slow the reader down.

Metaphor: saying that one thing is something else.

Imagery: helping the reader form a picture.

Repetition: repeating something with the same or similar words.

Rhythm: makes you tap your foot.

Simile: comparing, using like or as.

Personification: giving human traits to something that's not human.

Alliteration: using the same sound at the beginning of the neighboring word. "Debby did the deed."

Assonance: repetition of internal vowel sounds in words, such as ice, eyes, kite.

Onomatopoeia: words that sound like their meaning, such a cuckoo, swoosh, oink and sizzle.

Idiom: the use of common or colloquial sayings, such as a hot potato, the last straw.

Hyperbole: an exaggerated statement or comparison, such as "she was as big as a house."

Word Play: double meanings, (a favorite from Groucho Marx – if I said you had a beautiful body, would you hold it against me?), puns (she had a photographic memory but never developed it), and spoonerisms, a deliberate error in speech in which consonants or vowels are switched (is the dean busy becomes is the bean dizzy).

Poetry begins as a lump in the throat, a sense of wrong, a homesickness, a lovesickness.
Robert Frost

The Acrostic

We'll start our poetry exploration by creating an acrostic, a poem where each line begins with a particular letter. One familiar acrostic is from the poem/song by Howard Johnson, M-O-T-H-E-R. "M is for the million things she gave me . . . Put them all together, they spell MOTHER, a word that means the world to me." Probably not the most striking poetry in the world, but certainly words that have brought a smile to the lips of many a mother over the years.

The acrostic has been used for many centuries. There are a number of biblical examples, such as Psalm 119, an acrostic where each section begins with a letter of the Hebrew alphabet.

As another example, Edgar Allen Poe wrote the following acrostic poem in the 19th century:

An Acrostic

Elizabeth it is in vain you say
"Love not: - thou sayest it in so sweet a way
In vain those words from thee or L. E. L.
Zantipp's talent had enforced so well:
Ah! If that language from thy heart arise,
Breath it less gently forth – and veil thine eyesa
Endymion, recollect, when Luna tried
To cure his love – was cured of all beside
His folly, pride – and passion – for he died.

My Acrostic

List the letters of your name or a word of your choice down the left side of the page. Now write a poetic line that begins with each letter of your name or word.

Acrostic #1

Acrostic #2

The Haiku

The haiku is a Japanese form of poetry that uses very few syllables to paint a word picture. Its form is generally seventeen syllables in one line, or a three line poem of five syllables, seven syllables, and five syllables. Haiku often use sensory language to capture a feeling or image, often of the seasons or nature. It also usually contains some kind of juxtaposition, words or ideas that don't seem to belong together.

To write a traditional haiku, work through these three steps.

Step #1 Choose a subject and write down some of the words that come to mind on that theme.

Step #2 Organize your thoughts into three lines. Set the scene, and then expand on it by making an observation, expressing a feeling, or recording an action.

Step #3 Arrange your words into three lines (5-7-5). Substitute or rearrange words as needed.

Many haikus have a seasonal or nature reference. If possible, create a subject shift so that your poem has two parts. This has been described as "cutting," which places an imaginative distance between the two sections, each section enriching the understanding of the other. It helps to focus on a single mood or emotion. Also, using punctuation efficiently can improve a haiku.

Here's one example from the 1600s:

An old silent pond . . .
A frog jumps into the pond
splash! Silence again.
(Basho Matsuo)

Another example is more contemporary:

Whitecaps on the bay:
A broken signboard banging
In the April wind.
(Richard Wright)

A final example, using the form but not the seasonal theme, was written to connect the biblical narrative from Exodus 1 with the midwives in my life, both literal and figurative:

to Shiphrah and Puah

for a midwife: four haikus

breathe deeply, woman
mine the reservoir of strength
in jagged rhythm

labor on, sister
empower your straining womb
befriend its aching

let it birth, dear one
deliver up your riches
liberate promise

bare your breast, mother
let down the life-giving stream
milk to satisfy
(JoAnn Shade)

*Haiku is not a shriek, a howl, a sigh, or a yawn;
rather, it is the deep breath of life.
Santoka Taneda*

My Haiku Worksheet

Theme:

Line 1 (5)

Line 2 (7)

Line 3 (5)

My Haiku

My Haiku Worksheet

Theme:

Line 1 (5)

Line 2 (7)

Line 3 (5)

My Haiku

The Cinquain

A cinquain is a five-line poem with two main styles. The first is a poem that expands with the following pattern:

Line 1: one word for the topic
Line 2: two words to describe the topic
Line 3: three words that describe an action related to the topic
Line 4: four words that describe the feelings related to the topic
Line 5: one word that is another name for your topic.

Here's an example from a children's poetry class:

tree
white, tall
reaching, bending, fluttering
leaves and twigs, wind
aspen

A second style of cinquain is similar, with two syllables in line 1, four syllables in line 2, six syllables in line 3, eight syllables in line 4, and two syllables in line 5.

Here's an example of this second style of cinquain from Adelaide Crapsey, who created the form:

Look up . . .
From bleakening hills
Blows down the light, first breath
Of wintry wind . . . look up, and scent
The snow!

My Cinquain Worksheet (style 1)

Line 1: one word topic

Line 2: two word description

Line 3: three word action

Line 4: four words emotion

Line 5: one word synonym

My Cinquain

My Cinquain Worksheet (style 2)

Line 1: two syllables

Line 2: four syllables

Line 3: six syllables

Line 4: eight syllables

Line 5: two syllables

My Cinquain

The Limerick

A limerick is a five line poem in the AABBA form, meaning that the first, second and fifth line rhyme, as do the third and fourth. When we think of a limerick, it is usually with a smile, as they are often silly or funny.

Here's one example:

> There was an Old Man of Nantucket
> Who kept all his cash in a bucket,
> His daughter, called Nan,
> Ran away with a man,
> And as for the bucket, Nantucket.
> *(anonymous)*

My Limerick

Nonsense Poetry

Nonsense verse is a form of poetry that is whimsical and humorous in tone, and may use coined or meaningless words. One familiar nonsense poem is Jabberwocky by Lewis Carroll.

'Twas brilig, and the slithy toves
Did gyre and gimble in the wabe.
All mimsy were the borogoves,
And the mome raths outgrabe.
Beware the Jabberwock, my son!
The jaws that bite, the claws that catch!
Beware the Jubjub bird, and shun
The frumious Bandersnatch!

Here's Alice's reaction to the poem.

"It seems very pretty," she said when she had finished it, "but it's rather hard to understand!" (You see she didn't like to confess, even to herself, that she couldn't make it out at all.) "Somehow it seems to fill my head with ideas – only I don't exactly know what they are! However, somebody killed something; that's clear, at any rate."

The trick behind writing nonsense poetry like Jabberwocky is that it is composed from a language that is totally made up by the poet. That make-believe language gives the poem an air of other-worldliness.

1. Familiarize yourself with other nonsense poetry.

2. Follow the rules of English grammar.

3. Invent as many words as you want to stand in for English words. It should sound like it could be translated, but you don't need to know the meaning of all the words.

4. Establish the goal of your poem, so that it will tickle and satisfy the minds of your reader.

5. Write to create a new world with your language.

6. Let your ear tell you if it sounds finished.

7. Read it to children – see if they smile!

My Nonsense Poem

Free Verse

To conclude our poetry section, we'll try our hand at free verse, where patterns and rhyming are not required. Free verse can be rhymed or unrhymed, but it is written without the rules of meter. Sometimes the end of each line rhymes or uses slant rhyme, where words are similar in vowel or consonant, but don't fully rhyme. Some poets use full rhyming words or slant rhymes within each line.

Here's an example of slant rhyme from Emily Dickinson's pen. Notice that "soul" and "all" are a similar sound but not an exact rhyme.

> Hope is the thing with feathers
> That perches in the soul
> And sings the tune without words
> And never stops at all.

The absence of strict rules doesn't mean that anything goes. We still want to remember the poetry tools found on page 88, as well as the brain-storming process we used in the exercises at the beginning of this section. Choose words carefully, pay attention to punctuation, look for patterns and images, and don't be afraid to try new combinations of words and sounds.

How to start? Here's one way. Begin with a theme, an idea. Spend some time filling up a piece of paper with free-writing, similar to the idea of morning pages, of brain-storming. Don't erase or censor yourself. Get the ideas on paper.

Next, take your best ideas and images. Write them in paragraph form and read your words out loud. Note the places where you pause, where your lines naturally end. What words stand out to you? Try rewriting so your lines end with these emphasized words.

Now look at your draft. Take note of any rhymes. Count the syllables and circle sounds that repeat. Are there any patterns?

Try writing this in a different size and shape, such as shorter or longer lines, or replace some of the words with synonyms. Again, read it out loud, for a good poem should mimic the patterns of speech. As you massage your words, your poem will form a pattern that fits its ideas.

Free Verse Worksheet

Free Verse Worksheet

Creativity Tips from Donald Miller

1. A creator and his work are one.

2. Creators don't just talk about their work. They work.

3. A creator gets out of her own way.

4. A creator is ready when luck strikes.

5. Creators know their likes and dislikes.

6. Creators get rid of the takers in their lives.

7. A creator finds the rhythm and loves the rhythm.

8. A creator resists the urge to create out of anger.

9. A creator does not entertain hypotheticals.

10. A creator handles critics.

Sharing Words

Love, Friends, Money

Writing is like prostitution.
First you do it for love, then you do it for a few friends, then you do it for money.
Molière

For Self

When I write it feels like I'm carving bone.
It feels like I'm creating my own face, my own heart.
Gloria Anzaldua

We began this exploration with the goal of figuring out how writing could improve our mental and emotional well-being. While a number of studies claim there are benefits to writing, such as reduced doctor visits, increased productivity, and a lessening of depression, we were curious as to what difference it might make for ourselves. Now, in this last chapter, we begin by reflecting on whether writing has made a difference for us.

One benefit writing has provided to me is

One type of writing that I discovered I don't like is

My favorite writing exercise was

While the main priority of mental health counseling is to find resolution for problems and concerns facing the client, clients are encouraged to transfer the principles they learn to future situations. In the same way, you can pull out some of the ideas from these pages when you need to sort out concerns in the months ahead. And perhaps you've discovered an appreciation for both reading and writing words that will alter the rhythm of your days for many years to come.

For Others

Writing, like sewing, was always for someone, even if that someone was yourself in the future.
Writing was a way of sending your voice to someone you might never meet.
Margaret Atwood

Have you taken the plunge and shared your writing with others? Perhaps you began with your writing coach, a friend, or your counselor. When you first thought about letting others read your work, what were your emotions? Fear, excitement, shame, joy?

What have been some positive reactions?

Have you gotten any negative reaction? What has that felt like?

The artist doesn't have time to listen to the critics.
The ones who want to be writers read the reviews,
the ones who want to write don't have the time to read reviews.
William Faulkner

For Money – or at Least for Publication

When we write and are published, we become naked before people.
And that means we are open to criticism . . .
If you're going to write and get published, you've got to expect to have a few arrows thrown at you.
They're going to hurt, and you're going to bleed.
You're probably going to cry if you're like me.
But that's just part of it and you have to learn.
Madelaine L'Engle

Are you feeling the itch to get published? To share what you're discovering with the world? Your goal may not be the New York Times Bestseller List, but you've begun to develop a voice and you have something to say. So now what?

Here are some places to start:

- Susan Maccarelli's article, "Places to Publish Your Writing About Mental Health Topics," available on-line
- Your own blog or Facebook page
- Your local newspaper (op-ed, guest columnist)
- Your local mental health agency newsletter
- Your local mental health board's website or blog
- E-books (Nook Press, Kindle Direct Press)
- Self-published books (see createspace.com, lulu.com, nookpress.com)

Warning on self-publishing – some companies will try to see you services that you can perform for yourself – be wary!

One way I will share my writing with my community is

Practice Makes Perfect

It's easy to think about something we want to do, such as lose weight, paint the dining room, or become a writer. The challenge is to move from thinking about writing to doing it. Here are some thoughts on how to become a writer from those in the know.

If you wish to be a writer, write.
Epictetus

Writing is a matter of exercise.
If you work out and lift weights for fifteen minutes a day over the course of ten years, you're gonna get muscles.
If you write for an hour and a half a day for ten years, you're gonna turn into a good writer.
Stephen King

The only certainty about writing and trying to be a writer is that it has to be done, not dreamed of or planned and never written, or talked about (the ego eventually falls apart like a soaked sponge), but simply written: it's a dreadful, awful fact that writing is like any other work.
Janet Frame

I write when the spirit moves and I make sure it moves every day.
William Faulkner

I write all day; I don't have lunch out.
If you work every day, at the end of the year you have a book
Mary Higgins Clark

Writing is harder than anything else; at least starting to write is.
It's much easier to wash dishes.
When I'm writing I set myself a daily quota of pages, but nine times out of ten I'm doing those pages at four o'clock in the afternoon because I've done everything else first . . .
but once I get flowing with it, I wonder what took me so long.
Kristin Hunter.

Feedback

Feedback is essential for writers, no matter how much experience they've had. But it can also be devastating, especially when someone tells you that your "baby" is ugly. Here are some tips for handling feedback.

- Make sure your work is ready. Don't expect your friend or editor to do your work for you. Make any needed corrections first. Check spelling and grammar. Read your piece out loud to listen for rhythm and for missing words.

- Say thank you when someone has taken the time to read your first draft or to respond to your blog, column, or novel, even if the feedback isn't as positive as you wanted.

- Don't take it personally. A misspelled word is a misspelled word. An opinion is an opinion. It's not an attack on you (at least most of the time).

- Look for common themes in responses. Do two or three readers comment on the same ideas?

- Ask questions. What's missing? Can you connect with the characters? Does this make sense to you? Does this piece flow?

- Consider the source. If the feedback feels overly critical and you've gotten good response from others, it may be more about the reader than the piece. Say thanks, and then tell yourself, "That's one way of looking at it."

We are good and therefore we are capable of shining forth through our resistance to write well
and claim it as our own.
It is not as important for the world to claim it as it is to claim it for ourselves.
That is the essential step. That will make us content.
We are good, and when our work is good, it is good.
We should acknowledge it and stand behind it.
Natalie Goldberg

To Learn More

Journaling

mindyourmind.ca

Baldwin, Christina. *One to One: Self-Understanding Through Journal Writing.*

Cameron, Julia. *The Artist's Way: A Spiritual Path to Higher Creativity.*

Cameron, Julia. *The Vein of Gold: A Journey to Your Creative Heart.*

Loudon, Jennifer. *The Comfort Queen's Guide to Life: Create All That You Need With Just What You've Got.*

Progoff, Ira. *At a Journal Workshop: Writing to Access the Power of the Unconscious and Evoke Creative Ability.*

Ridgeway, Priscilla. *Pathways to Recovery: A Strengths Recovery Self-Help Workbook.*

Schaefer, Elizabeth Maynard. *Writing through Darkness: Easing Your Depression with Paper and Pen.*

Shade, JoAnn Streeter. *The Heartwork of Hope: A Directed Journal.*

Shade, JoAnn Streeter. *A Gentle Look Within: A Directed Journal.*

Shaw, Luci. *Life Path: Personal and Spiritual Growth through Journal Writing.*

Snow, Kimberly. *Writing Yourself Home.*

Thompson, Kate. *Therapeutic Journal-Writing: An Introduction for Professionals.*

Non-Fiction

Allison, Jay and Gediman, Dan, eds. *This I Believe: The Personal Philosophies of Remarkable Men and Women.*

Pipher, Mary. *Writing to Change the World.*

Ruszkiewicz, Friend and Hairston. *The Scott Foresman Handbook for Writers.*

Strunk, William and White, E.B. *The Elements of Style.*

Fiction

Bolton, Gillie. *Write Yourself: Creative Writing and Personal Development.*

Gardner, John. *The Art of Fiction: Notes on Craft for Young Writers.*

Goldberg, Natalie. *Writing Down the Bones.*

Goldberg, Natalie. *Wild Minds: Living the Writer's Life.*

King, Stephen. *On Writing: A Memoir of the Craft.*

Lamott, Anne. *Bird by Bird: Some Instructions on the Writing Lfe*

L'Engle, Madeleine. *Herself: Reflections on a Writing Life.*

Poetry

Behn, Robin and Twitchell, Chase. *The Practice of Poetry.*

Fox, John. *Poetic Medicine: The Healing Art of Poem Writing.*

Random House. *Rhyming Dictionary* (much more efficient than going through the alphabet in your head).

About the Author

JoAnn Streeter Shade, D.Min., has walked alongside others for more than thirty-five years, ministering in Salvation Army congregations and social service programs in New Jersey, Pennsylvania and Ohio, and at North Coast Family Foundation, a Christian counseling center in Northeast Ohio.

She is the author of more than twenty books in a variety of genres. She is a weekly columnist for the Ashland Times-Gazette and is a regular contributor to a number of Salvation Army publications. She is married to Larry, is the mother of three adult sons, Greg, Drew and Dan, and Lauren, a beloved daughter-in-law, and is Nana to the lovely Madelyn Simone and the delightful Elizabeth Holiday. She combines her academic training from Ashland Theological Seminary with a writer's eye, a pastor's heart, and a grandmother's joy through Gracednotes Ministries.

Contact her at gracednotesministries@gmail.com

Other Books By
JoAnn Streeter Shade

Heartwork of Hope: A Directed Journal

A Gentle Look Within: A Directed Journal

The Other Woman: Exploring the Story of Hagar

A Companion to the Other Woman: A Directed Journal

At the Bend in the Road: Reflections of a Smitten Corps Officer

Christmas Memories: Reflections of a Smitten Believer

Family Connections: Reflections of a Smitten Grandmother

Give It To Me Plain: Reflections of an Opinionated Lady

Only in Ashland: Reflections of a Smitten Immigrant

Seasons: A Woman's Calling to Ministry

Balm for the Wounded Healer

Rapha's Touch: Healing from Sexual Abuse

The Guerrilla and the Green Beret:
A Strategic Approach to Difficult Marriages

The God Gallery: Images of the Holy

WomenVoices: Speaking from the Gospels with Power

Holy Hunger: A Table Conversation on Holiness

Eliza: An Imagined Memoir (Eliza Duncan)

We Hear the Angels: Ancient Prayers for Advent

Questions of Advent for Christ-Seekers

Notes of Advent for Christ-Seekers

Faces of Advent for Christ-Seekers

Transformative Change (with Michael Misja)

Cooking With Love

Eliza and the Midwife: A Story in Human Trafficking

Made in the USA
Middletown, DE
02 September 2020

17577733R00071